How does a ship float?

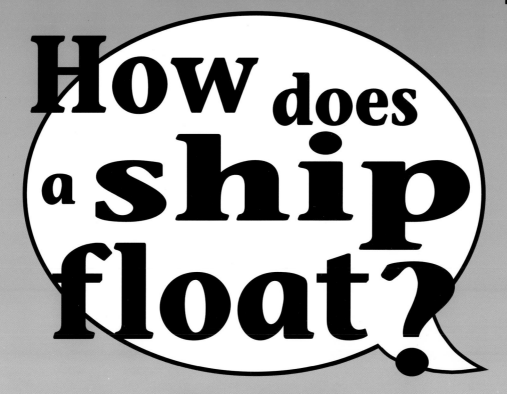

Jim Pipe

Copper Beech Books
Brookfield • Connecticut

Will the oar float?

It is a hot, sunny day. Amy and Steve are rowing around the pond. Amy's mom sits at the front of the boat. At the back, Zack watches the twigs float by.

Then Steve slips and drops his oar. What if it sinks?

Hang on to your oar, Steve, or it will sink!

Let's see how the children find out.

4

Look, the wooden block floats, even though it is heavier than the coin or the pebble!

It must float because it is made of wood. So a wooden oar must float, too.

3

Why it works

The block floats because it is made of wood. Wood and plastic float well because they are light for their size. That's why a wooden oar or boat floats well. Other materials are heavy for their size, like stone and metal, so even a small pebble or a coin sinks.

Solve the puzzle!

Can you tell what sinks and what floats? Put an apple, a candle, a safety pin, and an eraser into a bowl of water. Write down what happens. Then check your answers on page 22.

Why did the water splosh?

Phew! It's hot. Time for a swim. Amy's mom fills the pool to the top with water.

When the children sit down, the water sploshes over the edge of the pool onto the grass.

Oops! It must be the waves we made.

Let's see how the children find out.

As the tub gets lower, it takes up more space in the water.

Why it works

When you put something into water, it takes up space in the water. This pushes the water out of the way. The more space it takes up, the more water it pushes away. When lots of children get in the pool, lots of water gets pushed out!

3

Look at the mark, now. As the tub takes up more space, it pushes the water up more.

Solve the puzzle

Do things feel lighter or heavier in water? When you next have a bath, relax your arms in the water and see whether they feel heavy or light.

How does a ship float?

Next, the children play with their toys in the pool. Steve puts his metal boat in the water, and it floats. But when Amy puts in her car, it sinks to the bottom of the pool!

My boat is made of metal, but it still floats.

11

Let's see how the children find out.

It floats! The boat shape helps the clay to float.

3

Why it works

When Amy squeezes the clay into a boat shape it takes up much more space in the water. The more space an object takes up in the water, the more the water pushes against it and makes it float. A boat shape can make ships float even if they are made of metal.

Solve the puzzle

What boat shape can carry the most marbles without sinking? Find out by making different boat shapes from the same lump of clay.

13

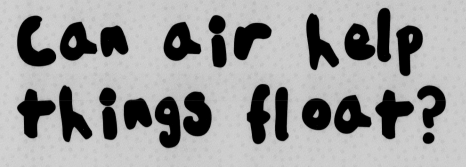

Can air help things float?

The next day the children go to the sea. Jo's dad is going to take them for a row, but first he blows up the boat.

15

Let's see how the children find out.

16

Why it works

Air is much lighter than water. So if something has air inside, it floats better. Air inside the can makes it float. It sinks because water pushes the air out, making bubbles. But Jo, Steve, and Zack are all correct about Jo's boat. Its shape, the plastic, and the air inside all help it to float.

Solve the puzzle

What happens when you push a soccer ball under the water and let go? Think about what is inside the ball.

Why is it easy to float in the sea?

The children go for a swim on a safe beach. "Who can float the best?" says Jo's dad, as he swims with the children. Jo shows the others how she can float on her back.

It's easier to float in the sea than in a pool!

19

Let's see how the children find out.

20

Why it works

Things float better in salty water because the salt makes the water heavier. The egg sinks because it is heavier for its size than water. When you add lots of salt to water, the salt makes the water heavier for its size than the egg, so the egg floats.

Solve the puzzle

Do ships float better in deep water? Fill a sink a quarter full of water. Put in a clay boat and mark on its side how high the water comes. Then fill the sink half full and check again. Does the boat float higher now?

Did you solve the puzzles?

Can you tell if something floats?

Look at this chart and check your answers:

Float	Sink
Apple	Safety Pin
Candle	Eraser

Are you surprised? Remember the wooden block on page 5. What matters is not how heavy something is, but how heavy it is for its size.

Do things feel lighter or heavier in water?

Your arms should feel lighter in water. Relax your arms so they drop into the water. Because your arms take up space in the water, it rises, just like water in the bowl on page 9. The water pushes up on your arms and makes them float, so they feel lighter.

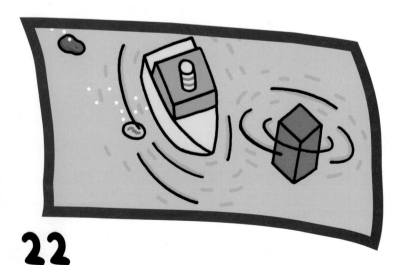

What shape carries the most marbles without sinking?

A deep, wide shape that takes up the most space in the water will carry the most marbles and still float.

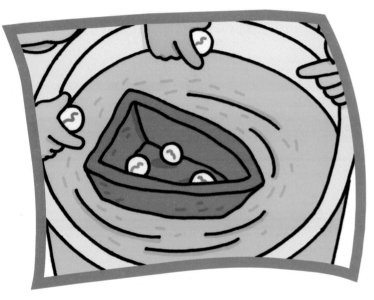

Do ships float better in deep water?

No. Your clay boat should float the same however full the sink is. Deep water makes no difference, even out at sea. Remember, like Jo, ships float better in the sea because of the salt in it.

What happens when you push a soccer ball under the water and let go?

The ball bobs to the surface. The air in it makes it float, like the can on page 17 when Steve blew air into it.

Index

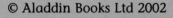

© Aladdin Books Ltd 2002

Designed and produced by
Aladdin Books Ltd
28 Percy Street
London W1T 2BZ

First published in
the United States in 2002 by
Copper Beech Books,
an imprint of
The Millbrook Press
2 Old New Milford Road
Brookfield, Connecticut 06804

ISBN 0-7613-2720-7 (Library bdg.)

ISBN 0-7613-1685-X (Trade h'cover)

Cataloging-in-Publication data is
on file at the Library of Congress.

Printed in U.A.E.
All rights reserved

Literacy Consultant
Jackie Holderness
Westminster Institute of Education
Oxford Brookes University

Science Consultant
Michael Brown

Science Testers
Ben, Toby, and Elliott Fussell

Design
Flick, Book Design and Graphics

Illustration
Jo Moore

For Clara Guerif

24